Love Is In The Air

by
SCHULZ

BOXTREE

Love Notes

You may not believe this, but

It Must Be Love

First published in 1997 by HarperCollins *Publishers* Inc. 10 East 53rd Street
New York NY 10022
This edition published in 1998 by Boxtree an imprint of
Macmillan Publishers Ltd 25 Eccleston Place London SW1W 9NF and
Basingstoke

Associated companies throughout the world.

ISBN 07522 21027

1 3 5 7 9 8 6 4 2

A CIP catalogue record for this book is available from the British Library.